FUNNY, WEIRD AND WISE THINGS LITTLE KIDS SAY

Fiona M Price

"What happens if you say my steak is at stake?" 7 yo

"Does this look really cute on me?" 3 yo

"How many years of uni do you need to do to work at laser tag?" 8 yo

I like to change my name every day. I call myself different things. My name was "coloured red" now my name is "nothing". 3 yo

"Can you drink wee ?" 8 yo

"We should burn people who test positive to Covid, problem solved!" 8 yo

Mum: "Please stop screeching"
Kid: "I've got human rights!" 8 yo

"God created the dinosaurs, and he realised their hands

were too far apart to pray so he deleted them." 8 yo

Mum: "You are so awesome, do you think I should make another baby?"
kid: "The other one might not be THIS good!" 7 yo

"How do I go about getting myself reincarnated?" 8 yo

Mum: "Put your dirty dish by the sink."
Kid: "If you don't clean up after me I will stop paying you in snuggles." 8 yo

Mum: "I said think about the neighbours"
Kid: "Did you just say to think about your anus?" 8 yo

'Why are animals and humans seen as separate?"8 yo

"I have a very big brain, a very deep brain deeper than other people. I was born with a big brain."8 yo

"If you think about it very deeply and think in terms

of survival, animals are more intelligent than humans. I don't think humans are intelligent because they let other people starve." 8 yo

"What's the point of the government? Hey, what if the government reads this? Well I control all the government as I'm a spy." 8 yo

Kid: "There are a billion copies of me. Actually I've lost count because they keep multiplying."

4 yo

"OMG you are so white you can't even pronounce names properly." 8 yo

"Fish are not fur babies." 6 yo

"I wish upon a star that I end up living with pirates." 3 yo

"You can't stop me from calling the cat a he." 8 yo

"I know why paper is white now, because of racism." 8 yo

"How many years of uni do you need to do to work at laser tag?" 8 yo

"Why does the moon not fall down from gravity?" 4 yo

"Why do the stars shine?" 4 yo

"I am going to take your computer when you die and all your money and my dad's money." 8 yo

"Can your brain handle this? Why are we here? Why does the universe exist?" 8 yo

"I told my dad that you hate fishing. That doesn't make sense though because you eat fish. So you are killing fish. Fishing & hunting is the natural circle of life." 8 yo

Kid: "I am not a vegetarian because I kill and eat animals." 4 yo

"Steve (aged 49) is a kid. Being a kid is a state of mind, not an age. Steve is silly and fun." 8 yo

"I could live without a mouth. It would be fun not having a mouth." 8 yo

"This is the bus Teddy, you have to tap on & tap off, if you don't they will come & take your toys." 4 yo

Mum: "I know some little boys your age in Beijing. Do you want to play with them?
Kid: "Do they speak English?"
4 yo

Mum: "You're growing up so quickly; before we know it, you'll be driving a car."
Kid: "Yeah, but where is my car?" 4 yo

"Grandma is the most beautiful woman in the whole world." 4 yo

"I want to have dunklings." 3 yo

"How does the earth rotate around the sun?" 3 yo

Kid: "Where do bears poop?"
Adult: "On the ground."
Kid: "Oh my god! Bears are terrible" 3 yo

"Is everything made of atoms?" 3 yo

Son: "Girls are too beautiful."
Mum: "Being a girl is not just about beauty, maybe on TV it is, but girls can also play sport, be strong and be a scientist"
Son: "I love girl scientists."3 yo

Son: "Do you find it hard not being able to take your shirt off in public?"
Mum: "Sometimes."
Son: "Then just become trans!" 8 yo

"No one is talking about climate change anymore. No one cares about pollution as corona is number one." 7 yo

"I don't want to get my eyes tested, I can already see, I can see okay." 3 yo

"If two people like you and are competing over you, why choose one person? That would make the other one lonely. Why not just choose neither of them and make them both lonely? I love torturing people." 8 yo

"If I get stranded on a desert island I will need a water purifier." 8 yo

"Once upon a time there was Dracula who wore black & lived in a house. He played with Play Dough & Lego." 3 yo

"Once there was a red lion with 100 fingers, she lived in a red triangle house with lots of play dough, she worked at McDonald's." 3 yo

"Have fish started to know about fishing yet? There should be a fish school to train them about fishing." 8 yo

Kid: "I wish the Illuminati take over the world, then the universe and then the galaxy."
Mum: "Where did you learn about that?"
Kid: "I've known since birth because I am part of them. Today I've been sticking triangles and eyes all over my classroom." 8 yo

Mum: "Can you come and help me with this?"
Kid: Sorry I have to be a cat for 24- hours." 7 yo

"Thank you very much. My mum told me to say that." 7 yo

Dad: "How was Melbourne?"
Kid:"There were lots of cars and mummy said shit." 4 yo

Dad: "How was Uluru?"
Kid: "Mummy said a bad word, a swear word, she taught me a new swear word." 5 yo

"There is that big pond." points at the Brisbane River. 7 yo

"Why do we grow taller every time the sun circles around the earth?" 7 yo

Mum sings: "It's beginning to look a lot like Christmas"
Kid: "It's not beginning to look like Christmas." 7 yo

Flew from Sydney to Brisbane.
"The people here look exactly the same as they do in Australia." 7 yo

"The future can change the past and the present right? If there was an error in the past it changes now? Is there even such a thing as the now?" 7 yo

"We are in the clouds! We are surrounded by whipped cream! We are in heaven!"
7 yo on a plane

Kid: What is the bible ?"
Adults: "It's a book that Christians believe was written by

God."
 Kid: "What!? They just found it? God just left it somewhere and they found it?
Adult: Well people wrote it but said that God told them what to write."
Kid: They can't prove that! I want to see this bible, I'll be able to tell if God wrote it. 7 yo

Song: "It's raining men"
Kid: (looks confused) "It's not raining men" 3 yo

"Is a reflection in a mirror an exact copy of reality?" 7 yo

"People have hands." 2 yo

"Bones in there." 2 yo pointing at his hands.

Kid: "What's Germany?"
Adult: "A country in Europe."
Kid: "On earth?" 2 yo

Harry put the tongs to his neck & said, "Eat Harry." 2 yo

"I'm not a thinker! I'm Harry." 1 yo

Kid: "Where are we?"
Mum: "Queen Victoria Building"
 Kid: "Where's the Queen?" 2.5 yo

"I'm going to have 20 babies." 3 yo

Kid: (afternoon) "I want to be a princess."
(morning) "I'm a tiger."
(midday) "I'm the baby." 2.5 yo

"I'm not going to dress up for Halloween as I'm scary the way I am." 6 yo

"I found a way to hack Into your phone." 7 yo

5am "I lived in your tummy when I was a baby." 2.5yo

Mum: "Do you think you look like mummy or daddy?"
Son: "I look like daddy because I'm not a girl" 2.5 yo

We moved house. "What is going to happen to the old place? Is someone going to come and smash it down with a wrecking ball?" 3.5y o

"The big lake is droughting." 7 yo

"Who is more popular? The boy government or the girl government?" 7 yo

Kid: "Call me coloured red."
Adult: "Okay, red."
Kid: "No, my name is 'coloured red'." 3.5yo

"Call me art man." 3.5 yo

Mum: "Mountain Pygmy Possum, critically endangered."
Son: "We have to rescue them!!!!" 2.5 yo

Son: "Have you ever had sex?"
Mum: "Yes."
Son: "What!!!???!!!" 6 yo

"God is God and Jesus is his girlfriend." 6yo

"Is it possible to defeat a dragon with a twig?" 7 yo

"It took ten weeks till the school holidays we should worship this day." 7yo

Kid: "Everything is multipurpose." 7 yo

Dad: "We are going on the train to the city."
Son: "Dinosaur train!! Dinosaur train!!!" 1 yo

Kid: "My friend Chris told me he lives in a mansion bigger than the school. Well, I own a mansion bigger than an entire planet." 7 yo

" I asked my dad, are you deep within the rabbit's fur on the edge of its bristles? My dad didn't understand, so I asked him, 'Are you comfortable with life and accept it as it is or do you question life and are a philosopher? Do you engage in deep thinking and ask questions that take unboundable years to answer?' My dad said he is a bit of both, but I think you are not a philosopher; you are deep within the rabbit's fur." 7 yo

"How are we here? Are we supposed to be here? Why are we here?" 7 yo

At 6am "How many Woolworths are there in the world?" 7yo

"You can control parents by calling kids helpline. If you don't give me chocolate, I'll call kids helpline." 7 yo

"I'm wind, I'm windy, I'm wind in the trees, I'm the tree falling down." 2.5yo

"I was in mummy's tummy, and I magicked myself into a baby." 2 yo

"You choke on an artichoke?" 3 yo

"My favourite thing about you is your money," 6 yo

Nightmare in his sleep "I want the black car." 3 yo

"If your head got chopped off and you were invincible, then you wouldn't be able to move your body, would you? I want to die by getting my head chopped off." 6 yo

"Wow, so light could travel around the earth 150 times in 20 seconds! Even if I was naked, I wouldn't be able to move around the earth that fast! You could blur me out so I could go fast." 7 yo

Kid: "What's that white stuff?"
Adult: "Moisturiser"

Kid: "Do you put that in your eyes?",
Adult: "No"
Kid: "Then why is it called moisture EYE ser?" 3 yo

Psychologist: "What's a way he can stay calm?"
Kid: "Stay asleep a long time so he can sleep and not wake up till he has a birthday party." 7 yo

Mum: "What can you say to the kindergarten kids to make them feel better on their first day at school ?"
Son: "I will tell them one million plus one million equals two million." 7 yo

"How do I know I'm not hallucinating?" 7 yo

"Today, we played poor people and rich people. I was the rich person earning $1000 a minute, and my other friends only had $1 and had to sleep on a park bench." 7 yo

Son: "Why are you always forcing me to do things?
Mum: "Because that's my job, I'm your mum. " 7 yo

"Everyone is a boy and a girl because if you chop off a doodle, you get a big gaping hole that is a vagina." 7 yo

Kid: "There could be life on other planets. Maybe they are

invisible?"
 Adult: "Well, Stephen Hawking thinks there is life on other planets."
Kid: "Of course!" 7 yo

Book: 'Earth is the only planet in the solar system to have life.'
Kid: "Well, they don't know that YET." 7 yo

Lilo (from Lilo & Stitch 2): "I'll never be like my mum. Maybe everything I do stinks."
Kid: "She needs to go to the psychologist." 7y o

"Facebook, that's just for old people." 7 yo

"In an art gallery, people could create their own abstract yoga poses, and that could be art." 7 yo

Adult: "Nothing is permanent."
Kid: "There are some things that are permanent. Air is permanent." 7 yo

Adult: "You can do anything!"
Kid:"Can I make it rain chocolate and then lick it off the

pavement?" 4 yo

"If you were as big as the whole world and you ate the world would you have to crunch it or not?" 7 yo

Kid "Did you know exercise makes you smart, it is good for your brain."
Mum: "Yeah."
Kid: "So I don't have to study anymore because I have an 8 pack." 7 yo

Kid: "What holds the thing that holds the galaxy?"
Mum: "Do you enjoy asking those big questions?"
Kid: "No it hurts my brain. I'm curious, I need to know, I can't just ignore big questions, I have to know even though it hurts my brain." 7 yo

"How many different realities are there? Is there a God for each different reality?" 7 yo

"If the galaxy holds the universe then what holds the galaxy? And what holds the thing that holds the galaxy?" 7 yo

"Thinking about time is a real brain hurter" 7 yo

Mum : "Don't lick the hand rail."
Kid: "You are making it more tempting." 7 yo

"Have I got a 7 pack because I'm seven ? Hey I've got an 8 pack! I keep growing more abs!" 7 yo

"Are we an animal? Are we an alien? How did we get created?" 7 yo

5.30am first words
Kid: "What is five times five hundred?"
Mum: 2,500
Kid: "I got my guess correct" 7 yo

"I'm a weird person. I'm a strange person you know." 7yo

Mum: "If you are rude to me in your next life your kid will be rude to you." Kid: "I'm not having kids in my next life." 7 yo

"You're a music lover, I'm a music hater." 7 yo

"Hey, why don't we just send all the Covid-19 positive people to North Korea and they can touch people?" 7 yo

"I am making plans to liberate North Korea." 7 yo

"Maybe god wanted the entire world to be one big country." 7y o

"But wasn't God on the Aboriginal people's side?" 7 yo

"That cat is going to the gym." 3 yo

Kid: "How can we learn more about black holes?"
Mum: "How do you think we can learn about them?
Kid: "Well I wouldn't want to jump into one as I may never get out." 6 yo

"Seeing that homeless man makes me really sad everyone should be rich." 6 yo

"When the common cold first came, was that really hard?" 6 yo

"Mum, don't lose weight because you might not look as good as you do now." 6 yo

Kid: "I spy something beginning with ch, train." 6 yo

"I can't believe we are a puzzle piece. Do you think some-one is jumbling us up right now and putting us back into place?" 6 yo

"Indonesia is both a girl and a boy." 6 yo

"Is Australia a boy?" 6 yo

Mum: "That's an orange hibiscus,"
Harry: "That's an orange Harry Biscuits?" 2 yo

Kid: "Your plate is covered in crumbs, and mine has no crumbs, nice and clean and fresh."
Mum: (looks under the table) " Your crumbs are all over the floor! Eat over your plate."
Kid: "But I like my plate being clean, fresh and crumb-free." 6 yo

"I'm seven, mum. I'm not a little kid anymore." 7 yo

Adult: "Why don't you become a YouTuber?"
Kid: "No, I want to become a booker and write books" 7 yo

The kid got up before me. I got up, and he said, "Did you get my note?" We went back to find the note on my bed. It said, "I got up." 7 yo

Mum: "The teacher said you are a role model of good behaviour for the other kids."
Kid: "Yes, that's because I can kill a kid with my own bare hands." 6 yo

"What if I get reincarnated onto another planet?" 6 yo

Kid: "Ha, you look like a baby like that."
Mum: "It's the child's pose."
Kid: "Why don't you do the adult's pose?" 5 yo

Kid: "A guy in my class hadn't heard about racism. He is black, and I told him about racism, and he has never heard of it."
Mum: "What did you tell him?"
Kid: "I told him racism is when people are against black or white people." 8 yo

"I rode a crocodile. It was a fine crocodile. It goes under-water and flies up in the sky. At night its eyes lit up like headlights. My seat flew up into the air when I pressed a button. There is a ladder so the crocodile can go into the sky." 3 yo

"I dig a hole, swim in the water, a crocodile eats me, I'm dead forever and ever, and someone comes to look for me." 3 yo

"This octopus is dead; now it comes back to life." 3 yo

"Why don't we put the pollution causing climate change into a black hole?" 7 yo

"Will the clouds turn into stars?" 3 yo

"At school, Sam said he would break my arm if I kept being annoying." 7 yo

"I would like it if we got an imaginary dragon and it snatched daddy up and made him have dinner with mummy and me." 4 yo

Pointing at KFC, "That is healthy", and then laughing

hysterically. 2 yo

Kid: "Why are owls nocturnal?"
Mum: They can see in the dark."
Kid: "Why?"
Mum: "They were just made that way."
Kid: They were made? Did someone make them? Every-thing was made by someone?"
3 yo

Kid re: screen time limits "Two hours is one hour be-cause one hour isn't very long." 7 yo

Mum: "There is no such thing as strangers, only friends you haven't met yet."
Kid: "Stranger danger." 6 yo

Kid: "Do you like Jakal Mikeson ?" (How he says Michael Jackson). 6 yo

Mum: "You were born in Sydney."
Kid: "Was I born in the Opera House?" 6 yo

Kid: "I'm going to wait until I'm 90 to become a teacher."
6 yo

Kid: "God won't be angry."
Adult: "Who is god?"
Kid: "God made the world in like one second. First, he made the trees, then humans, because if he didn't make the trees first, humans couldn't live." 6 yo

Mum was jaywalking.
Kid: "Don't break the law, be careful, or you will get addicted to breaking the law." 5 yo

"We should keep the Xmas tree up all year, so we don't have to put it up again. God won't be angry." 6 yo

"Everyone's brain is different. They see differently." 5 yo

"I have a fox brain, and I have purple neurons."   5 yo

"I wish I was fire." 4 yo

Mum: "How long do you think it will take you to get ready?"
Kid: "100 million years." 5 yo

"I'm going to learn all the languages in the world, first Chinese then American." 3 yo

"When I grow up, I want to have a girl & boy called Rosie & Starwars." 3 yo

"I feel social generally l between 2am - 8am."
 2 months old